Read for a Better World
Student Action and Reflection Guide

A Diverse Education

Today's world is ever changing and more closely connected than ever. To thrive in such a world, students need a deeper education than the memorization of facts and dates. They need to cultivate awareness, curiosity, and empathy toward themselves and the world around them. This guide helps grow and nurture the broad diversity of thought that kids need in our culturally diverse society. It is a first step in their journey to becoming citizens of a more just and collaborative world, but even more, it will build the skills they need to be architects of such a world.

About This Book

The activities in this book are inspired by the Social Justice Standards from Learning for Justice. They are organized by the American Association of School Librarians (AASL) Standards Framework for Learners. These frameworks were chosen because they emphasize inclusivity, student voice, and action.

How It Works

The student guide is divided into four chapters, each tied to an AASL domain: Think, Create, Share, and Grow. Chapters are subdivided into sections inspired by the four Learning for Justice domains: Identity, Diversity, Justice, and Action. These domains are called out with a colored tab in the upper corner of each page. Activities can be done in any order.

AASL Domains

THINK
Students learn to ask questions, think critically, solve problems, and gain understanding.

CREATE
Students learn to draw conclusions, make informed decisions, and apply knowledge to new situations.

SHARE
Students learn to share knowledge and participate as respectful and productive members of society.

GROW
Students learn to seek new knowledge, reflect, and pursue personal growth.

Learning for Justice Domains

Identity
Students reflect on their many identities, recognize the many identities of others, and practice expressing pride in their backgrounds while acknowledging and respecting where others come from.

Justice
Students learn to recognize unfairness and injustice, relate to people as individuals rather than representatives of groups, and identify figures and groups instrumental to the history of social justice.

Diversity
Students gain knowledge and language to accurately and respectfully describe how people are similar to and different from one another, building curiosity and empathy for the history and lived experiences of others.

Action
Students build and express empathy for others, recognize their personal role in acting against injustice, and reflect on ways they can speak up with courage and respect.

How We Celebrate ✳

Around the world, people celebrate holidays to honor special events. These holidays have special food, clothing, decorations, and more! Explore some celebrations around the world, and think about some of the ways your family celebrates special events.

Food

My holiday name: _____

When I celebrate it: _____

What the holiday celebrates: _____

_____

Foods I eat: _____

_____

Passover

Many Jewish people around the world celebrate Passover each spring. The holiday lasts one week. It celebrates the escape of the Jewish people from enslavement in ancient Egypt. Families gather together and eat a special holiday meal called a Seder. During the week of Passover, matzah is eaten instead of bread.

Pride Month

The month of June is Pride Month. All month long, people celebrate the LGBTQ community. Cities hold parades, festivals, and concerts in honor of Pride Month. People gather in city centers, in parks, and in their homes to show their support for the LGBTQ community.

LGBTQ: lesbian, gay, bisexual, transgender, queer

Gatherings

My holiday name: _____

When I celebrate it: _____

What the holiday celebrates: _____

_____

Where I go/where we gather: _____

_____

THINK

Decorations

My holiday name: _____

When I celebrate it: _____

What the holiday celebrates: _____

_____

How I decorate: _____

_____

diyas

rangoli

Diwali

In India, many people celebrate Diwali each fall. The holiday falls in October or November. The festival celebrates light overcoming darkness. People burn small lamps called diyas. Many people also decorate their homes with rangoli. These colorful designs are made of sand, rice, or flower petals and arranged on the floor.

Kwanzaa

From December 26 through January 1, many Black people in the United States celebrate Kwanzaa. This holiday honors the African heritage of many Black Americans. Kwanzaa has many symbols. Families light seven candles, one for each day. The candles symbolize the seven principles of Kwanzaa. The candles are placed in a special candleholder called a kinara.

Symbols

My holiday name: _____

When I celebrate it: _____

What the holiday celebrates: _____

_____

Symbols of my holiday: _____

_____

Identity

Outer Me

Your identity is made up of characteristics. Some are things people can see, such as the color of your skin or the texture of your hair. Other characteristics are the qualities people can't see, such as what you care about or believe.

What do people see when they look at you?

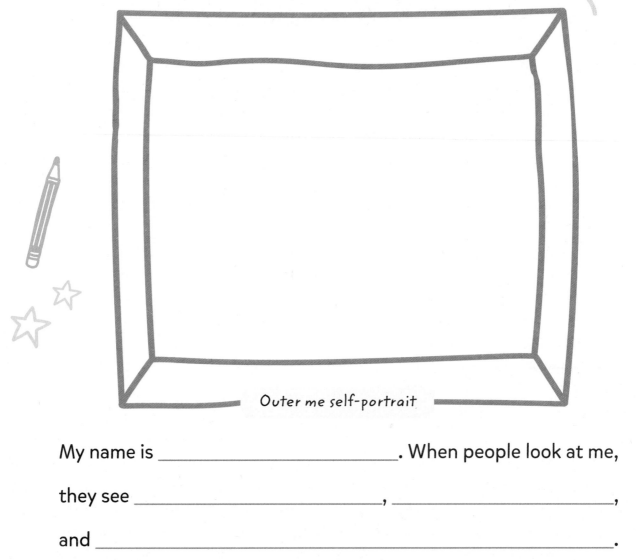

Outer me self-portrait

My name is _____. When people look at me,

they see _____, _____,

and _____.

Inner Me

What don't people see when they look at you?

Inner me self-portrait

My name is _____. I care about _____

_____.

I believe _____.

One thing people don't know about me is _____

_____.

Identity

Community Pie

You are part of many different groups. These groups can include the people at your synagogue, family, teammates, and many more. Think about some of the different groups you are part of. Fill in each section of the pie below with a symbol that represents what each group means to you.

Say It in Samoan!

Samoan is a Polynesian language that originated on the Pacific Islands of Samoa. Today, it is spoken throughout Polynesia.

Match Samoan words below with their English translations in the word bank.

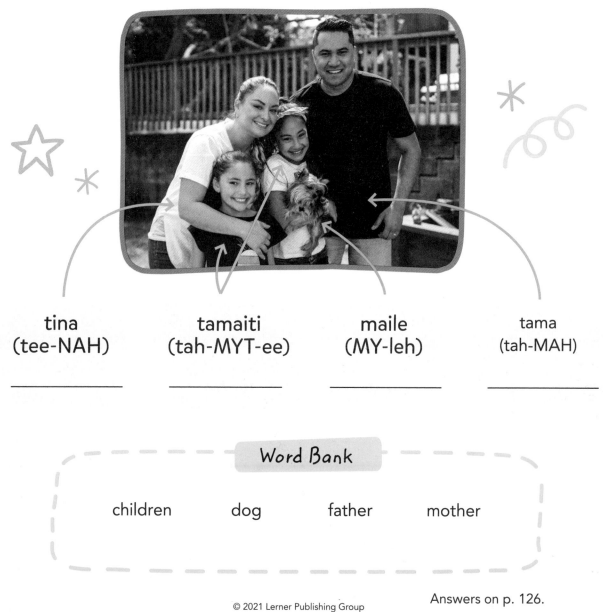

tina
(tee-NAH)

_____

tamaiti
(tah-MYT-ee)

_____

maile
(MY-leh)

_____

tama
(tah-MAH)

_____

Word Bank

children   dog   father   mother

Answers on p. 126.

Diversity

Winter Counts

Many Native peoples in North America's Northern Great Plains used winter counts to track important events in their communities. Each winter, communities would decide on one important event in the last year. The winter count keeper would draw a picture or symbol that represented that event. Circle the events below on this Nakota winter count from the 1800s.

Which symbol do you think represents a treaty? Why?

_____

_____

_____

_____

Which symbol do you think represents a meteor storm? Why?

_____

_____

_____

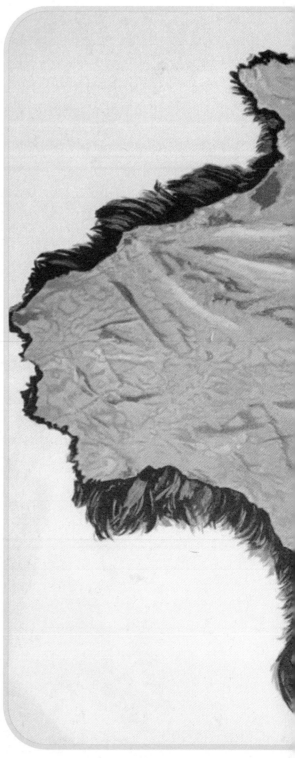

Answers on p. 126.

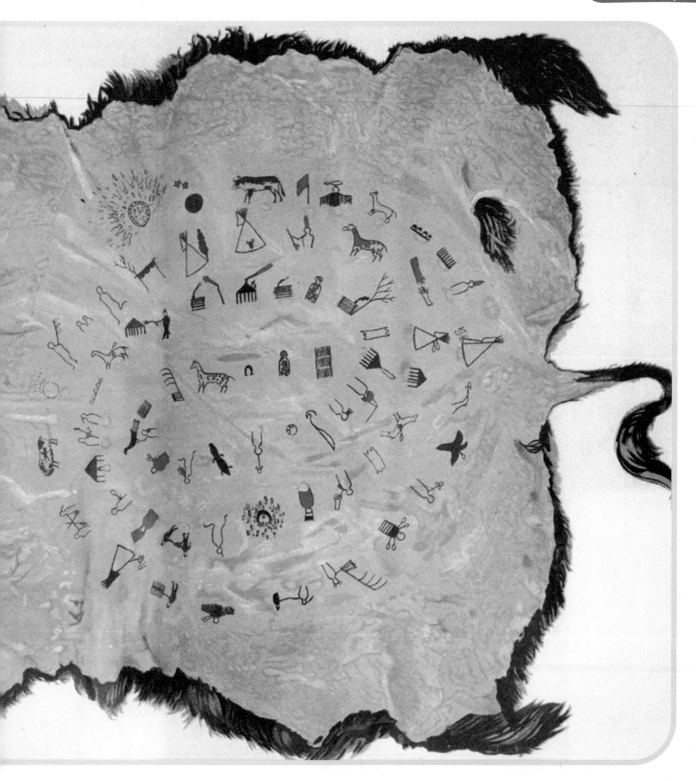

Diversity

Winter Count Interview

Design your own winter count, capturing some of the important events in your family. Interview family members to help decide which events are most important. Then fill out the chart below.

Year	Event	Symbol

My Winter Count

Turn the symbols from page 14 into a winter count!

Diversity

Celebrate Carnival!

Every winter, many parts of Central America, South America, and the Caribbean take part in a festival called Carnival. Carnival is loosely scheduled around the Christian season of Lent, when many Christians give up sugar, meat, or another luxury they may enjoy. Carnival celebrations are filled with music, dance, costumes, drums, and food! Learn about some of the Carnival traditions from different islands.

Trinidad and Tobago

Puerto Rico

These islands' celebration begins with a tradition called J'ouvert. People begin celebrating in the streets before sunrise. They cover one another's bodies in mud, chocolate, or paint.

This island's most famous Carnival celebration takes place in the city of Ponce. It begins with people wearing masks to represent vejigantes, spirits from Spanish folklore. The masked troublemakers try to playfully startle other partygoers.

Jamaica

Dominican Republic

Jamaica's main Carnival event is the National Carnival Road March. This parade through the city of Kingston features music, elaborate floats, costumes, and dancing.

Dominican Carnival has many parades with music, dancing, and costumes. People wear masks representing different characters from African and Spanish folklore.

Which Carnival festival would you most like to visit? _____

_____

Why? _____

_____

_____

_____

Diversity

((Carnival Costumes

Carnival in Rio de Janeiro, Brazil, is famous for its parade. Thousands of performers from Brazil's samba schools dance through the city. Each school has a different theme, called an enredo. Dancers from each school wear elaborate costumes tied to their school's enredo.

Enredo: Olímpico por natureza. Todo mundo se encontra no Rio!

Translation: Olympic by nature. Everyone is in Rio!

This samba school's enredo celebrates Rio de Janeiro hosting the 2016 Olympic games. How do you think the costume fits this theme?

_____

_____

_____

samba school: A Brazilian club for dancing, drumming, and marching

Carnival enredos can be based on people, places, events, and more. Write your own enredo below and design a costume to go with it!

My enredo: _____

_____

Food Staples

A food staple is a food that makes up a large portion of a diet for people in a given culture or community. Grains, tubers, roots, or cereals are food staples. Learn about some staple foods from different parts of the world.

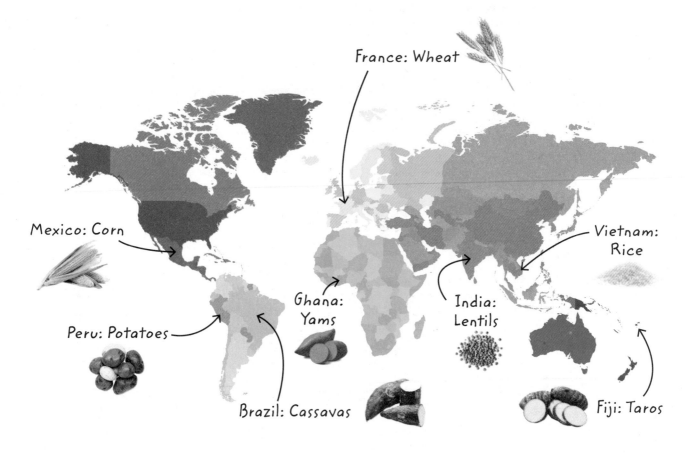

France: Wheat

Mexico: Corn

Peru: Potatoes

Ghana: Yams

Brazil: Cassavas

India: Lentils

Vietnam: Rice

Fiji: Taros

What is a staple food in your family or culture? _____

What are some ways your family enjoys this food? _____

_____

_____

My Family Recipes ♥

Create two recipe cards featuring a favorite family recipe that uses your food staple. List the ingredients on the front, then write the instructions on the back. Cut them out and give them to friends, classmates, or neighbors!

Recipe for: _____

Ingredients:

Recipe for: _____

Ingredients:

Instructions

_____
_____
_____
_____
_____
_____

Instructions

_____
_____
_____
_____
_____
_____

Color a Haida Drum

The Haida people live in North America's Pacific Northwest. Drumming is an important part of Haida music. Artists craft and decorate their drums with images from Haida culture and folklore. Traditional colors used are black, red, and green. Solve the math problems to color the drum below.

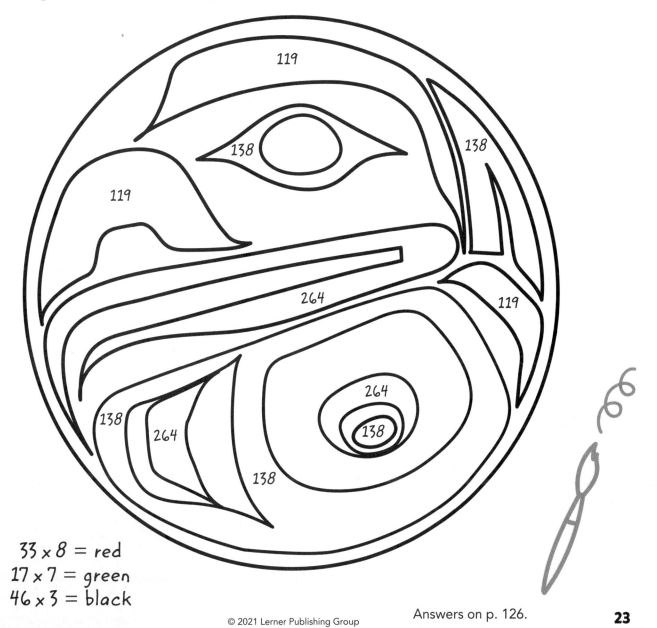

$33 \times 8 = $ red
$17 \times 7 = $ green
$46 \times 3 = $ black

© 2021 Lerner Publishing Group

Answers on p. 126.

Folktale Fun

Folktales are stories that are shared over many generations. These stories exist in almost every culture around the world! They can be funny, scary, or sad. Many folktales have morals, or lessons. In the past, these stories were almost always shared orally, or told aloud. Many cultures still share folktales orally. But now you can also read folktales in books or see them in movies or TV shows!

Think of a folktale you know. Write the folktale below and on the next page. Then answer the questions about your folktale.

_____

_____

_____

_____

_____

_____

_____

_____

_____

_____

_____

_____

_____

_____

_____

_____

_____

_____

Who is the main character of your folktale? _____

_____

What is the lesson or moral of your folktale? _____

_____

Diversity

Native Names

In 2015, the US government announced that it was officially changing the name of Alaska's Mount McKinley to Denali. This was the name the Koyukon Athabascan people had called the mountain for thousands of years. It means "the high one." Some other states and cities are also choosing to change the official names of local landmarks back to their Native names. Draw lines matching the Native names for famous national parks and monuments with their pictures.

Pa-hay-Okee means "grassy river" in Seminole

Geysers in Yellowstone National Park, Wyoming

Mato Tipila means "bear lodge" in Lakota

Devils Tower National Monument, Wyoming

Öngtupqa means "salt canyon" in Hopi

Everglades National Park, Florida

Bide-mahpe means "sacred or powerful water" in Apsáalooke

Grand Canyon National Park, Arizona

Answers on p. 126.

What's in a Name?

Names of places, such as streets, parks, buildings, and natural landmarks often reflect a community's unique history and culture.

Think about some of the names in your community. Then complete the activities below.

How are your community's unique history and cultures reflected in the names

of its places? _____

_____

_____

What history and cultures could be better represented in your community names? Come up with some new place names below!

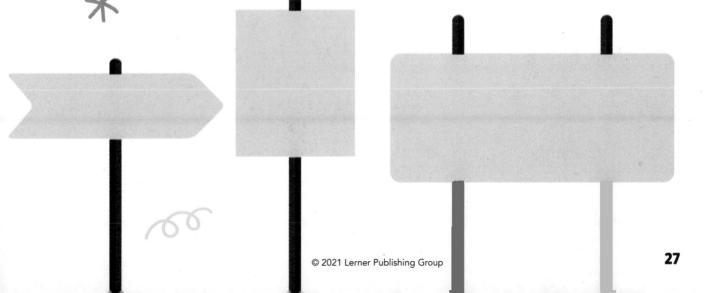

Take Action! Word Search

There are many ways to take action against injustice. Find some of these action words in the word search below.

```
K D E M O N S T R A T E J O
Q N J U E O R G A N I Z E C
F G E R A W E R Y M P N S H
B K I E D P E S S A N U T A
Y V B D L R Y F N T R N A L
V O E Q N O T M A U D I N L
T Q U E S T I O N T N T D E
K C X R Q E B P M J P I W N
C Q L S C S S P E A K G T G
M E E T O T O Z B A Y E C E
```

Words to find:

challenge	kneel	protest	stand
demonstrate	meet	question	unite
	organize	speak	

Answers on p. 126.

Is It Fair?

The US government has three branches. The legislative branch includes the House of Representatives and the Senate. The Senate has 100 members. This includes two representatives from each state. The House has 435 members. The number of representatives from each state depends on that state's population. States with more people have more representatives. The House and the Senate must work together to pass bills. If a bill is approved by both the House and Senate, it goes to the president. If the president approves the bill, it becomes a law!

Why do you think the Senate has two representatives from each state and the House's representatives are based on a state's population?

_____

_____

_____

Do you think having people work together to make laws makes them more

fair? Why or why not? _____

_____

How does your family make rules? _____

_____

_____

THINK

The Same but Different

Everybody is unique! Getting to know someone as an individual can give you a better idea about who they are. The best way to get to know people is by asking questions. Think about a person you would like to know more about. This could be a classmate, friend, neighbor, or family member. Fill out the first two columns in the chart below.

What I know	What I want to know	What I learned
My big sister makes TikTok dance videos.	Why did my sister make her first video?	My sister made her first video to wish her best friend happy birthday!

Interview the person you chose, using the questions in the second column. Then fill out the third column with what you learned.

✶ Is It Fair? ✶

The US government has three branches. The legislative branch includes the House of Representatives and the Senate. The Senate has 100 members. This includes two representatives from each state. The House has 435 members. The number of representatives from each state depends on that state's population. States with more people have more representatives. The House and the Senate must work together to pass bills. If a bill is approved by both the House and Senate, it goes to the president. If the president approves the bill, it becomes a law!

Why do you think the Senate has two representatives from each state and the House's representatives are based on a state's population?

_____

_____

_____

Do you think having people work together to make laws makes them more

fair? Why or why not? _____

_____

How does your family make rules? _____

_____

_____

The Same but Different

Everybody is unique! Getting to know someone as an individual can give you a better idea about who they are. The best way to get to know people is by asking questions. Think about a person you would like to know more about. This could be a classmate, friend, neighbor, or family member. Fill out the first two columns in the chart below.

What I know	What I want to know	What I learned
My big sister makes TikTok dance videos.	Why did my sister make her first video?	My sister made her first video to wish her best friend happy birthday!

Interview the person you chose, using the questions in the second column. Then fill out the third column with what you learned.

Think about what you learned from your interview.

What do you and the person you interviewed have in common?

_____

_____

What makes the person you interviewed unique? _____

_____

_____

_____

What did you learn about the person you interviewed that surprised you?

_____

_____

_____

Justice

Angelou Analogy

Maya Angelou was a writer and Civil Rights activist. She wrote many books, essays, poems, and plays. Angelou's work has been praised for celebrating Black culture while portraying it in an authentic way. Like many poets, Angelou often used analogies to help her readers see things from a new perspective. An analogy shows how two things are alike. Read the analogy from her poem "Still I Rise" below:

> You may write me down in history
>
> With your bitter, twisted lies,
>
> You may trod me in the very dirt
>
> But still, like dust, I'll rise.
>
> —Maya Angelou

What two things is Angelou comparing in her analogy? _____

_____

In what ways are they alike? _____

_____

Now, write your own analogy! _____

_____

_____

_____

The Power of Pronouns

A pronoun is a word that can take the place of a noun in a sentence. Examples of pronouns include *his*, *him*, *her*, *she*, *their*, and *they*.

It is important to use correct pronouns. If you aren't sure of someone's pronouns, ask which ones you should use.

Circle the pronouns in the sentences below. Then, write a sentence about yourself using your pronouns.

Emmitt is the goalie for their soccer team. Every morning, they get up early to practice with their team. Last week, they blocked a goal at the last second to win the game!

Malia raises chickens in her backyard. Every morning, she lets them out of their coop and makes sure they have enough food and water.

Cai loves cooking. His favorite recipe to make is hot sauce. He even grows his own chili peppers!

About Me

_____

_____

_____

  Answers on p. 126.

Meet Indya Moore

Indya Moore is an actor, model, and activist. Read a short biography of Moore and their accomplishments. Then, answer the questions on the next page to reflect on what you learned.

Indya Moore

Indya Moore was born in New York City in 1995. Moore was assigned male at birth. But they identify as female nonbinary. Moore's parents did not support their identity. So, Moore left home at age 14. They went into foster care, where they were frequently bullied.

When Moore was 15, they began modeling. In the 2017, Moore was cast as a lead in the in the award-winning show *Pose*. In the show, Moore plays a transgender character. In 2019, Moore became the first transgender model to appear on the cover of *Elle* magazine.

Moore believes in using their fame to help others. They use social media and give speeches promoting LGBTQ and anti-racist causes. Moore has spoken out against unfair treatment of transgender people, including cisgender actors playing transgender roles. In 2020, Moore started a charity to provide Christmas gifts for transgender youths.

Where was Indya Moore born? _____

_____

What causes does Moore support? _____

_____

_____

What does Moore do to show their activism for LBGTQ rights? _____

_____

_____

_____

Do you think it is important for transgender actors to play transgender roles?

Why? _____

_____

_____

Why might people consider Moore to be influential? _____

_____

_____

_____

Answers on p. 126.

Action

Journal for Change

The first step toward making the world a better place is knowing that you have the power to make a difference. For example, if you care about the environment, you could encourage people in your school to recycle by making signs. Think about a cause you care about. Write a journal entry about the cause and how you could take action to make a difference!

_____

_____

_____

_____

_____

_____

_____

_____

_____

I Am an Activist!

Think about a cause you care about and how you could become an activist for that cause.

A cause I care about is _____

because _____

_____.

I show I care about this cause by _____

_____

_____.

I can convince others to care about this cause by _____

_____

_____.

Identity

Mini Graphic Novel

Many families have true stories they like to share again and again. Think about a favorite family story. It may be one you lived through or a story from before you were born. Illustrate the panels below and on the next page to create your own mini graphic novel of this story!

Use the panels below to set the scene. Show where the story begins and who is present.

Now introduce the main conflict. What event leads to the climax of the story?

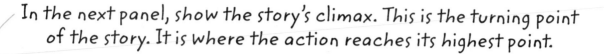
In the next panel, show the story's climax. This is the turning point of the story. It is where the action reaches its highest point.

Next comes the falling action of the story. What happens after the climax? How do the characters resolve the conflict?

In the last panel, show how the story ends.

Identity

My Timeline

Use the space below to create a timeline of your own life. Write out eight important events, starting with your birth. Include one or two events you hope will take place in your future. Draw pictures in the open frames!

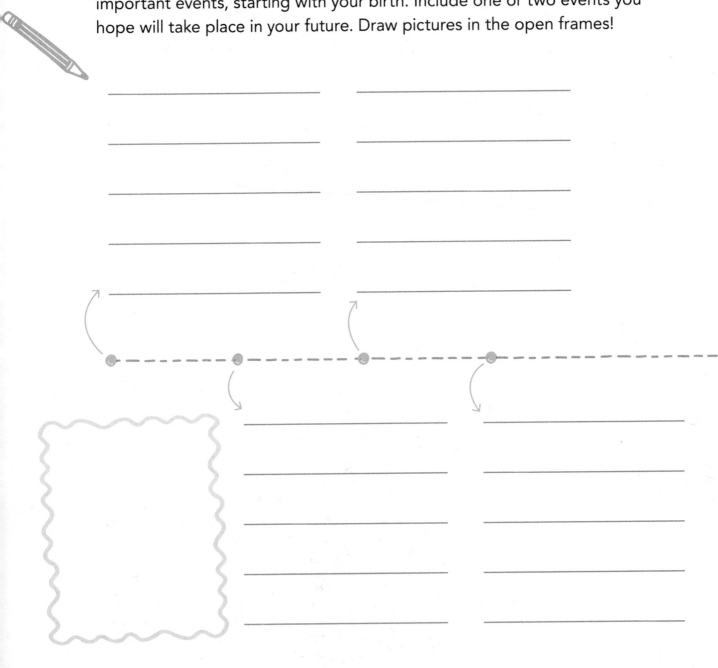

Where I Live

Think about the city or town you live in. Answer the questions about it below.

I live in _____.
                                    (city/town)

It is in _____. People in this city/town speak
                    (country)

_____.
                                    (languages)

Something I like about my city/town is _____

_____.

One challenge my city/town faces is _____

_____.

I would like to help my city/town be better at _____

_____.

Draw a place
in your city or
town where
you like to visit.

Mind Map

We all go through each day with many different things on our minds. What's on yours? Maybe it's a certain food you've been craving. Maybe it's a basketball game you're feeling nervous and excited about.

Create your mind map below by drawing and labeling some of the things on your mind at this moment.

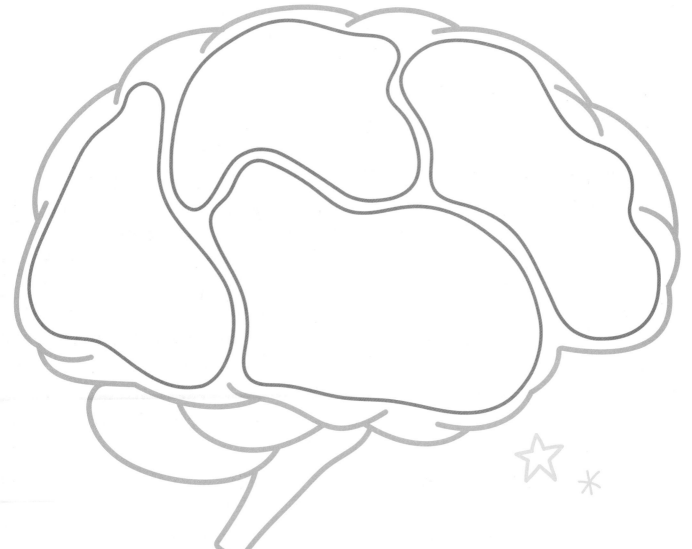

Self-Portrait

Mexican artist Frida Kahlo was known for her self-portraits. She once said she painted self-portraits because "I am the person I know best." Kahlo channeled her life's pain and joy into her paintings.

Do you think you are the person you know best? Why or why not?

_____

_____

_____

Create your own self-portrait in the frame. Choose an emotion you would like the self-portrait to depict.

What emotion did you choose to depict in your self-portrait?
How did you show the emotion?

_____

_____

_____

_____

_____

Sonia Sotomayor

Sonia Sotomayor was born on June 25, 1954, in New York City. Her parents were from Puerto Rico. Sotomayor went to college at Princeton University in New Jersey. She then attended Yale Law School in Connecticut.

Sotomayor became a US District Court judge in 1992. Five years later, she was nominated to the Court of Appeals for the Second Circuit. President Barack Obama nominated Sotomayor to the Supreme Court in 2009.

On August 8, 2009, Sotomayor became the 111th Justice of the Supreme Court. She was sworn in by Chief Justice John G. Roberts Jr. at the Supreme Court Building in Washington, DC. Sotomayor was the first Hispanic justice to serve on the court. She was also only the third woman to do so.

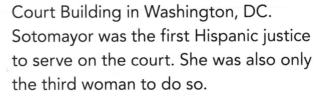

On the next page, fill in the key points about Sonia Sotomayor becoming a Supreme Court Justice. Then draw a picture to go with what you wrote.

WHEN did the event happen?_____

_____

WHO was involved? _____

_____

WHAT happened?_____

_____

WHERE did it happen? _____

WHY did it happen?_____

_____

_____

_____

WHY will this event be remembered in history?

_____

_____

_____

_____

_____

Answers on p. 126.

Climate Map

Africa is a continent of more than fifty countries. It is the second-largest continent on Earth. Below is a map showing different climate regions in Africa. Use the map to answer the questions on the next page.

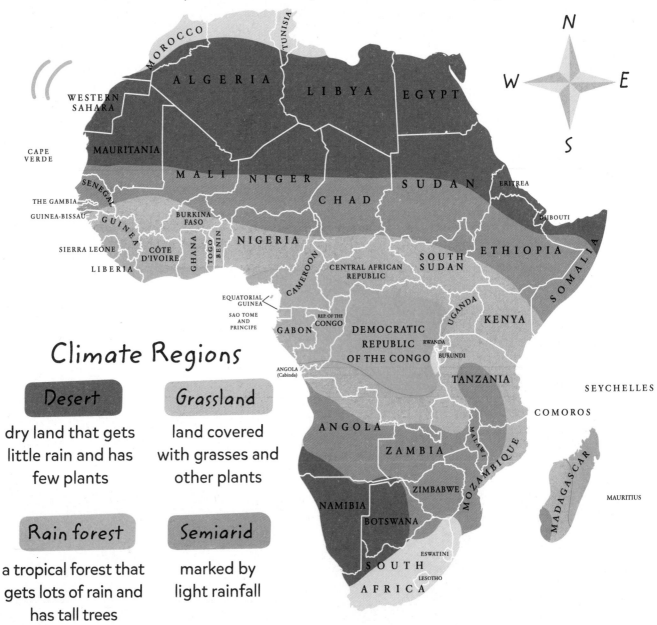

Climate Regions

Desert
dry land that gets little rain and has few plants

Grassland
land covered with grasses and other plants

Rain forest
a tropical forest that gets lots of rain and has tall trees

Semiarid
marked by light rainfall

© 2021 Lerner Publishing Group

What is the largest climate region in the northern part of Africa?

_____

Which country includes two different climate regions, Gabon or South Sudan?

_____

Which country includes three different climate regions, Ethiopia or Liberia?

_____

Which country includes a rain forest climate, Ghana or Zimbabwe?

_____

Which country includes a desert climate, Uganda or Somalia?

_____

Name the largest climate region in Mauritania.

_____

Name the largest climate region in
the Central African Republic.

_____

Answers on p. 127.

Ramadan Fast

Ramadan is a holy month for Muslims. During Ramadan, most adults fast from sunrise to sunset. This means they do not eat or drink. Ramadan is a time to practice good behavior and self-reflection.

Fasting during Ramadan is a type of sacrifice. In many different religions, people give things up on special occasions. This helps them to focus on what is important. It is also a way to practice discipline.

Think about something you could give up. Maybe it is eating candy or drinking soda. Maybe it is playing video games. Then answer the questions below.

Muslims often break their fast by eating dates.

What could you give up? _____

What could you do in place of what you are giving up? _____

_____

How do you think you would benefit from making this sacrifice? _____

_____

_____

Celebrating Eid al-Fitr

After Ramadan, there is a festival called Eid al-Fitr. Eid al-Fitr means the Festival of Breaking Fast. It begins at the end of Ramadan.

To prepare for Eid al-Fitr, families clean and decorate their homes with lights, candles, and banners. They make cakes, cookies, and other sweet treats. During Eid al-Fitr, Muslims pray, eat meals with family and friends, and exchange gifts.

Think about a holiday your family celebrates. Answer the questions about it below.

My family celebrates _____.

To prepare for this holiday, we _____

_____.

Some foods we make for the holiday are _____

_____.

We celebrate the holiday by _____

_____.

Navajo Code Talkers

The Navajo are a Native American people of the southwestern United States. During World War II, a group of Navajo men joined the US military. Their job was to create a code based on the Navajo language. The code allowed US troops to send important messages. Enemy forces were unable to break the code!

In the key below, every letter of the alphabet is assigned a symbol. Use this key to create a coded message on the next page. Then have a friend or family member decode the message by looking at the key!

Code Key

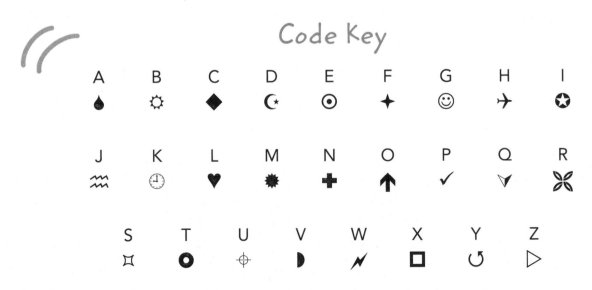

Coded Message

Decoded Message

Native Dwellings

Hundreds of Native American and First Nation tribes lived in North America before European settlers arrived. These tribes used the natural resources around them to build shelters. The style and materials of a shelter were influenced by the land and climate around it.

Match the different types of shelters below with the tribes that built them. Use the tribe's location as a clue for what kinds of natural resources would be available to build shelters.

cypress logs
and palm branches

Algonquin
(Northeast)

Cheyenne
(Great Plains)

buffalo hide and
wood poles

birch bark

Haida
(Northwest)

Hopi
(Southwest)

packed snow

dried clay

Inuit
(Arctic)

Seminole
(Southeast)

cedar wood

Answers on p. 127.

Design a Dwelling

Design a shelter based on the climate and landscape you live in. Think about what natural resources would be available to you. Include those materials in your design!

Nelson Mandela Day

Nelson Mandela was an activist in South Africa. Starting in the 1940s, he fought against apartheid. This was a system that kept Black and white South Africans separate. Under apartheid, Black people did not have the same rights as white people.

Nelson Mandela helped end apartheid. He became president of South Africa in 1994. Today, people celebrate Nelson Mandela International Day on Mandela's birthday, July 18.

Think of someone in your life who has worked hard to make life better for others. Create a holiday in honor of that person. Make a sign for the holiday that includes the following:

- Name of holiday

- Date of holiday

- Image or symbol that represents the holiday

Jackie Robinson Timeline

Jackie Robinson is an American baseball legend. He was born on January 31, 1919, in Cairo, Georgia. His full name was Jack Roosevelt Robinson. His parents were Jerry and Mallie Robinson.

In 1939, Robinson began attending college at the University of California, Los Angeles (UCLA). He participated in football, track and field, baseball, and basketball at UCLA.

In 1945, Robinson joined the Kansas City Monarchs, a baseball team in the Negro Leagues. Two years later, he began playing for the Brooklyn Dodgers. This made him the first Black player in Major League Baseball in the twentieth century.

Robinson retired from baseball in 1957. He was inducted into the Baseball Hall of Fame five years later. In 1963, he and his wife Rachel hosted a jazz concert to raise money for jailed Civil Rights activists. Robinson co-founded Freedom National Bank in 1964. The bank became the largest Black-owned and operated bank in New York state.

On October 24, 1972, Robinson died of heart problems. He is remembered as a baseball hero, barrier-breaker, and activist.

Organize the key events in Jackie Robinson's life on the timeline below, starting with his birth. Include the year of each event.

_____

_____

_____

_____

_____

_____

_____

_____

Richard Wright's Haiku

Richard Wright was a celebrated Black writer. He was born in Mississippi in 1908. Much of Wright's writing was about being a Black American. Near the end of his life, Wright composed thousands of haiku, many about the beauty of the natural world.

The sudden thunder

Startles the magnolias

To a deeper white.

This autumn evening

Is full of an empty sky

And one empty road.

Heaps of black cherries

Glittering with drops of rain

In the evening sun.

Whitecaps on the bay:

A broken signboard banging

In the April wind.

What do Wright's haiku have in common? What themes do you notice?

_____

_____

_____

_____

_____.

Haiku are made up of three lines: the first has five syllables, the second has seven syllables, and the third has five syllables. Compose your own haiku using this structure.

_____

_____

_____

Flint Water Crisis

In 2014, Flint, Michigan, began dealing with a water crisis. The city's water was unclean and unsafe to drink. Many people argued that because most Flint residents were Black, the water crisis was an example of environmental racism. In March 2016, Flint resident Mari Copeny decided to take action. The 8-year-old wrote a letter to President Barack Obama about the crisis in her city.

Obama responded to Mari's letter, saying he would be visiting Flint to address the water crisis. Mari got to meet Obama during his visit. After that, she continued speaking out against environmental racism. She helped raise hundreds of thousands of dollars to bring clean water to the people of Flint and around the world.

In the spring of 2021, the city of Flint was still working to replace pipes. There were still residents without clean water. They needed to use water filters to make sure their water was clean.

environmental racism: the disproportionate impact of environmental hazards on people of color

Mari hugging President Barack Obama in Flint, Michigan, in 2016

Mari wrote a letter to the US president to address a problem in her community. What is a problem you know about in your city, region, or country? Who could you write to about the problem? Use the space below to write your letter. Then cut it out and send it!

Dear _____,

_____

_____

_____

_____

_____

_____

_____

_____

CREATE

_____

_____

_____

_____

_____

_____

_____

_____

Sincerely, _____

What's Your Cause?

People often wear buttons or badges that advertise a cause they care about. What is a cause you believe in? Maybe it's recycling or supporting local farms. Maybe it's adopting rescue animals.

Create a badge for your cause below. Then cut it out and wear it to show others what you believe in!

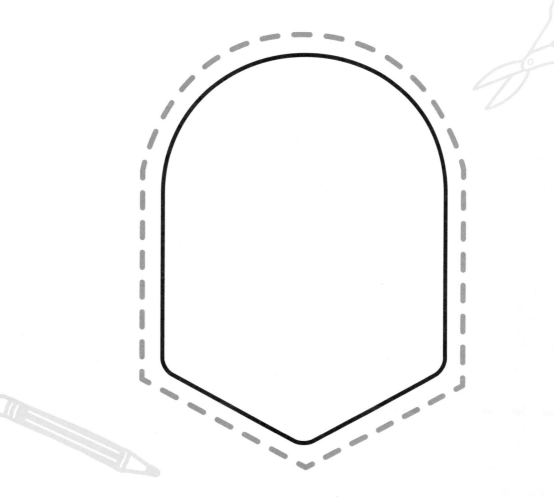

Action Word Search

There are many ways you can make your voice heard. Find some of these actions in the word search below.

```
K M U G Y D H W D T E G M A
C W R I T E O S S P E A K D
Q T A Y B F A R O N B P O E
U B C Z W E S A N B R L E K
E O R G A N I Z E N E E B L
S Y B M V D P K W E P S P E
T C I U P G Z W E S O N R A
I O B N A L Q R X N R V O R
O T X N F K W F P P T B T N
N T F P W O N Z L J R O E R
P J Z E M F R G A S I Z S W
C M E N K J C M I N P B T R
O D C H A L L E N G E I N S
```

Words to find:

boycott
challenge
defend
explain
inform
learn
organize
protest
question
report
speak
write

Pick one of the words from the word search and share how you can take that action to fight discrimination.

_____

_____

_____

 Answers on p. 127. **67**

Identity

Where We Come From

People around the world migrate for many reasons. Some migrate because the place where they live is no longer safe. Others migrate to be close to family or friends. People may also migrate in search of better opportunities for work, education, or quality of life.

A Southern Black family arrives in Chicago in 1920

Groups often migrate from one country to another. For example, many people living in the United States migrated from Mexico, India, and other countries.

People also migrate within the same country. One of largest US migrations was known as the Great Migration. Between 1916 and 1970, more than six million Black Americans migrated from rural areas in the South to large cities in the Northeast, Midwest, and West. These cities offered more opportunities for higher paying jobs.

What is your migration story? Has your family lived in your community for a long time, or are you new to the area? Answer the questions about your family history below. If you don't know the answers, ask a family member.

How long has your family lived in your community? _____

_____

Where did your family or ancestors live before? _____

_____

Why did they move? _____

_____

_____

Draw a map or picture showing your family's migration story.

My Mission Statement

A mission statement is a declaration of the beliefs and goals of a group. A school could have a mission statement declaring what kind of learning environment they want. A group of doctors may follow a mission statement declaring how they believe patients should be treated. Members of a social movement may follow a mission statement declaring their goals for creating change.

What is your mission statement? Make your own declaration by filling in the blanks below!

I believe that _____

_____.

Every day, I try to _____

_____.

Someday I hope to _____

_____.

Growing and Learning

As we grow up, we learn to do new things. What are some things you have learned to do over time? What do you hope to do in the future?

Things I can do now that I couldn't do before:

_____   _____

_____   _____

_____   _____

_____   _____

_____   _____

Things I can't do now but hope to do in the future:

_____   _____

_____   _____

_____   _____

_____   _____

Words to Inspire

Mae Jemison was the first Black woman to be an astronaut. She speaks Russian, Japanese, and Swahili, in addition to English. She also founded two technology companies!

Jemison once said, "Never limit yourself because of others' limited imagination."

Using your own words, share what you think this quote means.

_____

_____

_____

_____

_____

_____

Mae Jemison lives by the advice she gave. What is a piece of
advice that you have found helpful? Share the advice here.

_____

_____

_____

_____

_____

_____

Think of a situation in your life where you can apply the advice above.
Share your thoughts here.

_____

_____

_____

_____

_____

_____

Practice Hebrew!

Hebrew is a language spoken in Israel and in many Jewish communities around the world. The Hebrew alphabet looks different from the English alphabet.

ה	ד	ג	ב	א
He	Dalet	Gimel	Bet	Alef

י	ט	ח	ז	ו
Yod	Tet	Chet	Zayin	Vav

ס	נ	מ	ל	כ
Samech	Nun	Mem	Lamed	Kaf

ר	ק	צ	פ	ע
Resh	Qof	Tsadeh	Peh	Ayin

			ת	ש
			Tav	Shin

Did You Know?

- The Hebrew alphabet has 22 letters.

- Hebrew is written and read from right to left.

- Outside of Israel, the United States has the largest Hebrew-speaking population in the world.

Below are words written in English and then Hebrew. The Hebrew words include pronunciations using English letters. Practice saying the Hebrew words!

English	Hebrew
hello	שָׁלוֹם (sha-LOM)
goodbye	לְהִתְרָאוֹת (le-hit-ra-OT)
snack	חָטִיף (kha-TIF)
one	אַחַת (a-KHAD)
two	שְׁתַּיִם (SHTA-im)
three	שָׁלוֹשׁ (sha-LOSH)
four	אַרְבַּע (AR-ba)
five	חָמֵשׁ (kha-MESH)

Of the words you just practiced, which one is your favorite to say?

_____

What is another word you would like to learn in Hebrew? Share how you could

find out the Hebrew word. _____

_____

Then and Now

Interview an adult family member. Ask them the following questions about what life was like for them growing up. Write their answers in the space below each question.

After they've answered every question, think about your own answer to each question. Write your answer on the second line.

1. How did you get to and from school?

Their answer: _____

My answer: _____

2. What was your favorite subject in school?

Their answer: _____

My answer: _____

3. How did you communicate with friends outside of school?

Their answer: _____

My answer: _____

4. What did you and your friends do for fun?

Their answer: _____

My answer: _____

5. What was a common family meal you ate?

Their answer: _____

My answer: _____

Compare your answers to the adult's answers. How was their experience growing up similar to yours? How was it different? Share your thoughts here.

_____

_____

_____

_____

_____

Facts and Opinions

Discussions about climate change are full of facts and opinions. Can you tell the difference between the two?

Read the statements below. Write 'F' next to the facts and 'O' next to the opinions.

fact:
a statement that is proven through research.

opinion:
something you think or feel. It cannot be proven, and it often varies from person to person.

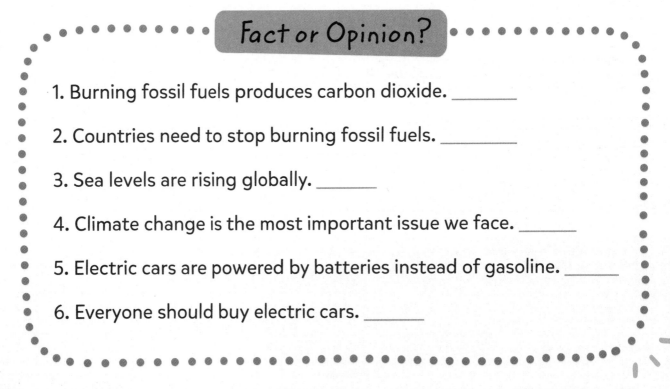

Fact or Opinion?

1. Burning fossil fuels produces carbon dioxide. _____

2. Countries need to stop burning fossil fuels. _____

3. Sea levels are rising globally. _____

4. Climate change is the most important issue we face. _____

5. Electric cars are powered by batteries instead of gasoline. _____

6. Everyone should buy electric cars. _____

Answers on p. 127.

Indigenous Peoples' Day

Indigenous Peoples' Day takes place on the second Monday of October. The holiday was first proposed in 1977 as a replacement for Columbus Day, which honors the Italian explorer Christopher Columbus and his arrival in the Americas. But Columbus and other colonists like him brought violence and death to Native populations. Many Americans argued that celebrating Columbus ignored and disrespected the history of Indigenous communities.

Some American cities and states honor Indigenous Peoples' Day instead of Columbus Day. Indigenous Peoples' Day recognizes the first inhabitants of the Americas and honors their resilience against the violence of European explorers.

Indigenous Peoples' Day became a holiday because communities acknowledged a problem and took action to make a change. Can you think of a time a community you are part of initiated a change? Share what happened below.

_____

_____

_____

_____

Taking a Knee

In 2016, pro football player Colin Kaepernick began kneeling during the US national anthem as it was played before games. Most players stood for the anthem. Kaepernick kneeled as a form of protest. He was protesting the oppression of Black people and people of color in the United States.

Kaepernick's actions sparked a movement as more and more players began kneeling during the anthem.

Kaepernick appeared on a Nike ad that said, "Believe in something. Even if it means sacrificing everything."

Some people thought it was unpatriotic to kneel during the national anthem. Others thought it was patriotic to call attention to problems in one's country. What do you think? Explain your answer.

_____

_____

_____

_____

Some people thought national football games were not the right place for protests. Others thought football players had a right to use their platform to share their beliefs. What do you think? Explain your answer.

_____

_____

_____

_____

Kaepernick risked his football career and public image to take a stand against racism in his country. What is one way you can take a stand against injustice in your community? What risks come with this action? What gains? Share your thoughts.

_____

_____

_____

_____

_____

Justice

Inner and Outer Selves

We all have parts of our lives and personalities that we are happy to share with others. But there are usually some things that we keep to ourselves.

Things my friends and classmates know about me:

_____

_____

_____

_____

_____

_____

_____

_____

Things my friends and classmates may not know about me:

_____

_____

_____

_____

_____

_____

_____

_____

What is something you would like others to know about you that they don't already know? How could you share this part of you with them?

_____

_____

_____

_____

_____

Think of a classmate you know little about. What would you like to know about this person?

_____

_____

_____

_____

_____

_____

_____

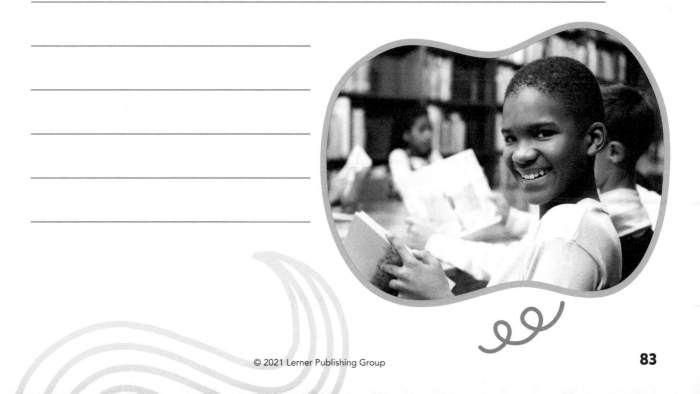

Justice

All Are Welcome

When you are a member of a group or community,
it's important to make new members feel welcome.

Think about a time when you were new to a group or community. What did people do or say to make you feel welcome?

_____

_____

_____

_____

What could you do to show a new classmate that they are welcome?

I could invite them to _____.

I could tell them about _____

_____.

I could show them how to _____.

I could give them a _____.

I could ask them about _____

_____.

Communities are stronger when they are welcoming to everyone. Color the sign below. Then cut it out and hang it where people can see it!

85

Spell It Out

What does fairness mean to you? Spell it out with an acrostic poem!

In an acrostic poem, the first letters of all the lines combine to form a word. Below, start each line of your poem with a letter from the vertical word FAIRNESS. Use the lines of your poem to describe what fairness means to you.

F _____

A _____

I _____

R _____

N _____

E _____

S _____

S _____

Justice

Kamala Harris

Kamala Harris made history in 2021. She became the first female vice president of the United States. She was also the first Black American and the first South Asian American to hold the position.

In a speech, Harris said it was an honor to "stand on the shoulders of those who came before."

Before becoming vice president, Harris served as attorney general and later senator of California.

What is exciting about being the first to do something?

_____

_____

_____

_____

_____

What is hard about being the first to do something?

_____

_____

_____

Think about Harris's quote on the previous page. Who do you think she was talking about when she said "those who came before?" What do you think it means to "stand on their shoulders"?

_____

_____

_____

Do you think it's important that the leaders of a nation come from many different backgrounds and perspectives? Why?

_____

_____

_____

Juneteenth

Juneteenth is a holiday that celebrates the end of enslavement in the United States. It takes place on June 19th. On this date in 1865, Union General Gordon Granger arrived in Galveston, Texas. There, he informed enslaved Black Americans that the Civil War had ended and they were free. This was more than two years after President Abraham Lincoln had issued the Emancipation Proclamation.

Communities across the nation celebrate Juneteenth with parades, barbecues, and other festivities.

The enslavement of Black Americans is a shameful part of US history. Do you think it is important that Americans remember and reflect on this time? Why?

_____

_____

_____

_____

_____

Juneteenth Word Search

Find all the ways people celebrate Juneteenth in the word search below!

```
U A Q H I D P W V C E B J O S P H
H W M U S I C S M P E A K D T O K
L T A Y E B N K I R N S O E R E P
V D C Z R E D V E L V E T C A K E
B O B G A O I B K N E B Y L W B L
X Y O B V D D K W E P A P E B Y E
Q P I U P G Z E E S O L O D E R A
G O A N A L Q R O N R L B R R O R
O T X R F K O T P C T B T N R T O
B T F P A O U N L J R P R A Y E R
P J Z E M D R G A S I Z S W S S R
C M B A R B E C U E P B N R O E R
Y D C W I P L B N Z E I E I D R A
I D C Z F I S H I N G I N S A N M
```

Words to find:

barbecue   music   red velvet cake

baseball   parade   rodeo

fishing   prayer   strawberry soda

 Answers on p. 127.

Cesar Chavez

Cesar Chavez was a Mexican American activist born in 1927. Chavez fought for the rights of farm workers from the 1960s until his death in 1993.

Chavez used nonviolent protest to fight for change. For example, California grape pickers worked in poor conditions for low wages. So Chavez asked Americans to boycott the grapes. Workers also took part in marches and nonviolent strikes. Because of these protests, farm workers eventually received better pay and benefits.

Cesar Chavez at a United Farm Workers rally in Delano, California, in the 1970s

Why do you think boycotting a certain product or company works to make positive change?

_____

_____

_____

_____

Do you think it's important to keep protests nonviolent? Why?

_____

_____

_____

Imagine you learned your favorite brand of shoe was made by workers who were treated poorly. What is one way you could respond in protest?

_____

_____

_____

_____

Action

Taking a Stand ☺ ♡ ♥

History is full of heroes who took a stand for what they believed in.

Rosa Parks took a stand by staying seated on a bus.

Cesar Chavez took a stand by organizing boycotts and strikes.

Colin Kaepernick took a stand by kneeling during the national anthem.

What are some other ways people can peacefully stand up for what they believe in? List your ideas below.

_____

_____

_____

_____

_____

_____

Think about a time when you took a stand for a cause you believed in. What did you do? What did you say? How did you feel? Share your thoughts about the experience below.

_____

_____

_____

_____

_____

_____

_____

_____

_____

Respecting Differences

We all have different perspectives. A perspective is a viewpoint or way of seeing something. Our perspectives are shaped by our individual experiences.

You may have different perspectives from your friends and classmates. You can show respect for someone's perspective by listening to them and asking them questions about their views.

Think of a time you and a friend, classmate, or family member had differing viewpoints about something. What was your perspective?

_____

_____

_____

_____

What was the other person's perspective?

_____

_____

_____

Did you feel like the other person respected your perspective? Why or why not?

_____

_____

_____

Did you show respect for the other person's perspective? If so, how? _____

_____

_____

_____

_____

_____

Mindfulness Break!

Mindfulness means being aware of what is happening in the present moment. This includes noticing any emotions you are feeling, physical sensations, and the world around you. Answer the questions below to capture the moment you are living in right now!

Right now...

Physically, I feel: _____

Emotionally, I feel: _____

I see: _____

I smell: _____

I hear: _____

Yoga incorporates mindfulness and breathing. It comes from a Hindu tradition that dates back thousands of years. People across the world practice it today for physical and mental well-being.

You can do a little bit of yoga just about anywhere. Find an open space where you feel comfortable, and follow the instructions on the next page to give yoga a try!

1. Sit or stand in a comfortable position with your arms at your sides.

2. Take a deep breath in through your nose. Then let the breath travel back out of your mouth.

3. The next time you breathe in, raise your arms up on either side of your body. Keeping the arms straight, let your hands meet above your head as you finish inhaling.

4. As you breathe out, slowly lower your arms until they are back at your sides.

5. Breathe in and out twice more, moving your arms with your breath.

6. For your last three sets of breaths, raise your chin along with your arms. When you inhale, bring your chin up toward the sky. When you exhale, move your chin down toward your chest.

These movements feel more natural the more you do them. Now that you've finished, how do you feel? _____

_____

_____

_____

Identity

Mindfulness Journal

You can practice mindfulness by taking a few minutes each day to really focus on your environment and your emotions. For the next week, spend five minutes each day answering one question.

Day 1

Write about the place where you feel safest and happiest. Why do you think it makes you feel this way?

_____

_____

_____

_____

_____

Day 2

What gives you confidence to try something new? Why?

_____

_____

_____

_____

Day 3

Who are the people in your life that you are most grateful for? Why?

_____

_____

_____

_____

_____

_____

Day 4

What emotions do you experience when you accomplish a challenging task? How do you feel when you are working through a difficult task?

_____

_____

_____

_____

_____

_____

GROW

Day 5

What emotions are you feeling right at this moment?
What emotions did you experience earlier today?

_____

_____

_____

_____

_____

_____

_____

Day 6

What parts of your life make you happiest? Is there any way
you can spend more time doing these things?

_____

_____

_____

_____

_____

_____

Day 7

What does it mean to be a strong person?
What makes you strong?

_____

_____

_____

_____

_____

_____

_____

Reflection

Now that you've finished a week of journaling, reflect on what you learned!

What did you enjoy most about journaling? _____

_____

What did you find most challenging? _____

_____

What did you learn about yourself? _____

_____

Identity

Finding My Strengths

Many different qualities make you *you*. You have skills. These are things you do well. You also have character traits. These are the qualities that make you who you are. Character traits can include kindness, generosity, and honesty. In the space below, list the character traits and skills you are proudest of.

My Character Traits

My Skills

How do your character traits and skills help you achieve your goals or overcome challenges? Write a journal entry explaining your answer!

_____

_____

_____

_____

_____

_____

_____

_____

_____

Meet Serena Williams

Serena Williams is a professional tennis player. Many people believe she is one of the greatest athletes of all time. Read the bio of Williams below, and answer the questions on the next page.

Serena Williams

Serena Williams started playing tennis at age four. She was athletic and strong. She trained hard. She was determined to win. When Williams was sixteen, she started playing tennis professionally. In 1999, she became the second Black woman to win a Grand Slam title.

As Williams's fame grew, she spoke out against the way female players were treated differently than male players. She also spoke out against the racism she experienced in the mostly white sport. When the media reported unkind things about the way she looked, Williams was confident in herself. She was proud of her African heritage and her athletic body. She encouraged others to take pride in themselves as well.

Williams has won two Olympic gold medals and more Grand Slam titles than any other modern tennis player in history. She has taken time off to heal from injuries and have a baby, but she has never given up! She has also tried to make the world a better place. Williams puts her wealth to good use by investing in businesses owned by Black women.

How did Williams' skills and character traits help her overcome the challenges

she faced? _____

_____

_____

What do you admire most about Williams after reading her biography?

_____

_____

How do your skills and character traits help you overcome challenges?

_____

_____

What might people admire about you?

_____

_____

_____

Mandala Meditation

A mandala is a geometric figure. It is a spiritual symbol in both Hindu and Buddhist cultures. The mandala represents wholeness and the universe. People create mandalas as a way to meditate and connect with the universe.

Color in the mandala below. Take the opportunity to let your mind relax while you focus on the colors and design of the mandala.

Celebrate Spring

Every spring, Japan's cherry trees blossom in beautiful flowers. The blooms remain for only one or two weeks before withering. During this period, people take part in a tradition known as hanami, or "flower viewing." Family and friends gather in parks to take walks and enjoy picnics below the blossoms. Hanami celebrates and honors the natural beauty of spring.

Do you celebrate a holiday that marks the start of a new season?

If so, what holiday? _____

_____

What role does nature play in your celebration of this holiday?

_____

_____

_____

Famous Firsts

Pioneers are people who are the first to do something. Match the names and pictures of the pioneering women below with their amazing accomplishments on the next page.

A — Sonia Sotomayor

B — Deb Haaland

C — Mae Jemison

D — Ali Stroker

E — Aretha Franklin

F — Amelia Earhart

What does it mean to be a pioneer? _____

_____

How could you be a pioneer? _____

_____

Have you ever been the first in your family to do something? If so, what was it like? _____

_____

——

First woman to fly a plane solo across the Atlantic Ocean

——

First Hispanic justice to serve on the US Supreme Court

——

First woman to be inducted into the Rock & Roll Hall of Fame

——

First Black woman in space

——

First actor who uses a wheelchair to win a Tony Award

——

First Native American to serve in a US president's cabinet

Answers on p. 127.

Poetry Power!

Amanda Gorman is the youngest poet to read at a US presidential inauguration. In January 2021, she read a poem at the inauguration of President Joe Biden. Read the excerpt from her poem, "The Hill We Climb," below:

When day comes we ask ourselves,
where can we find light in this never-ending shade?
The loss we carry,
a sea we must wade.
We've braved the belly of the beast,
We've learned that quiet isn't always peace,
and the norms and notions
of what just is
isn't always just-ice.
And yet the dawn is ours
before we knew it.
Somehow we do it.
Somehow we've weathered and witnessed
a nation that isn't broken,
but simply unfinished.

Gorman delivered her poem during a time when the United States was dealing with a pandemic, racial injustice, political unrest, and economic hardship. What are some words Gorman uses that hint at those struggles?

_____

_____

_____

What does the line "quiet isn't always peace" mean to you? _____

_____

_____

Gorman plays with the words "just is" and "justice." What do you think is the difference between the two? _____

_____

_____

Gorman says the nation is not broken, but simply unfinished. What do you think it means for a nation to be unfinished? _____

_____

_____

Justice

Origami Cranes

In 1945, when Sadako Sasaki was just two years old, the United States dropped atomic bombs near her home in Japan. Sadako was exposed to the bombs' radiation. As she got older, this radiation made her very sick. According to Japanese legend, if a person folded 1,000 origami paper cranes, they would be granted a wish. When Sadako was twelve, she began folding paper cranes from her hospital room. She didn't have origami paper, so she folded them from medicine wrappers, gift wrap, and papers her friends brought from school. Sadako went on to fold 1,300 paper cranes. She died soon after. But her story lives on. Sadako's story helped bring attention to the long-term consequences of the bombing.

A statue of Sadako stands in Seattle, Washington.

Follow the instructions to make your own paper crane!

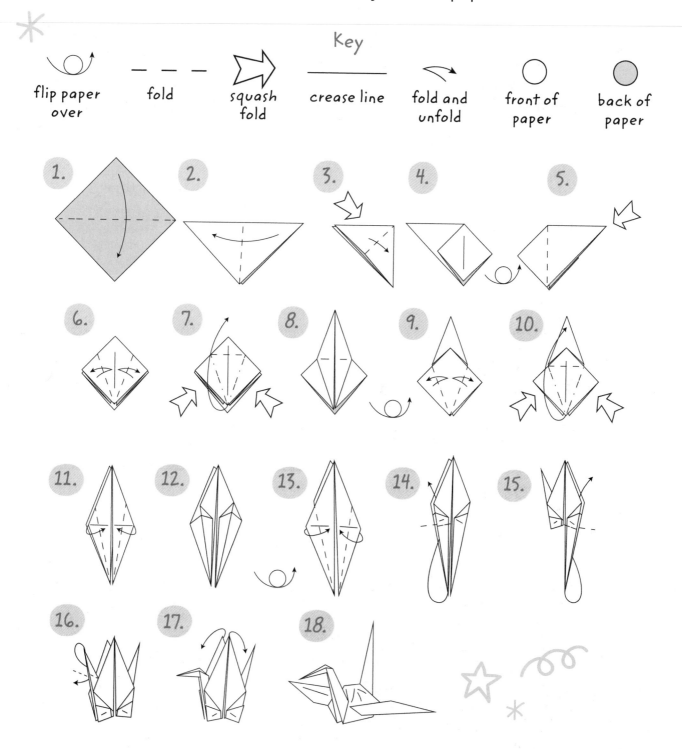

Key

flip paper over — fold — squash fold — crease line — fold and unfold — front of paper — back of paper

1. 2. 3. 4. 5.

6. 7. 8. 9. 10.

11. 12. 13. 14. 15.

16. 17. 18.

Justice

Two Views

Every issue has at least two sides. Practice thinking about one question from two different points of view by filling in the two different responses to the questions below. Make sure to provide reasoning for each answer.

Many social media sites, such as TikTok and Instagram, require users to be thirteen to make an account. Should younger kids be allowed to make accounts?

Yes, because _____

_____

_____

_____

_____ .

No, because _____

_____

_____

_____

_____ .

Should kids be allowed to bring smartphones to class?

Yes, because _____

_____

_____

_____

_____.

No, because _____

_____

_____

_____

_____.

Should schools require kids to wear uniforms?

Yes, because _____

_____

_____

_____

_____.

No, because _____

_____

_____

_____

_____.

Marley Solves a Problem

When Marley Dias was eleven years old, she noticed unfairness in her school. Most of the books she was assigned to read featured white boys. Marley felt this was unfair. She wanted Black girls like her to have the opportunity to read books featuring characters that looked and acted like them. Marley started a campaign called #1000BlackGirlBooks. Her goal was to collect 1,000 books starring Black girl characters. The campaign went on to collect more than 13,000 books! It also drew attention to the diversity missing from children's books. Marley's activism helped make reading more fair for everyone.

What is something you find unfair in your community? _____

_____

Now think of a possible solution to help correct this unfairness: _____

_____

_____

What are some steps you could take to make

Marley Dias

this solution a reality? _____

_____

_____

_____

A New Community

You might belong to many different communities, such as an art club, sailing team, church group, or neighborhood cleanup crew.

Write down some communities you are part of. _____

_____

Now, write down a community you would like to be part of.

_____

_____

Why would you like to be part of this community? _____

_____

_____

Write down what steps you can take to join or start this community.

_____

_____

_____

Raise Your Voice!

Think about a cause you care about. It could be related to animals, the environment, or social justice. Why is this cause important to you? Why should other people care about it? What do you think could be done to help the cause? Make notes in the space below. Then, use the next page to turn your notes into a two- to three-minute persuasive speech. This is a type of speech where the speaker tries to convince the audience of something. Practice giving your speech in front of a mirror first. Then try giving it to your family or friends! Were they persuaded to care about your cause?

Speech Notes

Speech title:_____

_____

_____

_____

_____

_____

_____

_____

_____

_____

_____

Action

#MakeADifference

Small actions can make a difference! In 2013, people across the United States began using the hashtag #BlackLivesMatter on social media. The hashtag called attention to the unfair treatment of Black Americans. The hashtag soon spread around the world! It started the Black Lives Matter, or BLM, movement. Today the movement works to fight racism and promote equal treatment, and to stop violence against Black people.

What cause do you want to draw attention to? _____

_____

_____

_____

Why is this cause important to you? _____

_____

_____

Use the space on the next page to design a social media post to draw attention to your cause. Make sure to include a hashtag, text, and an image that will catch people's attention!

Action

Repair and Grow

Have you treated someone unfairly or said hurtful things? Have you seen someone be treated unfairly and not spoken up? It takes courage and humility to admit when we are wrong, and to apologize for what we did. But doing so makes us bigger and better than we were before. Saying sorry helps us grow!

Asking questions can be a great place to start when working to repair harm that was caused:

- What happened?

- What was I thinking and feeling at the time?

- Who was impacted?

- What would help make things right?

Read the scenarios on the next page. Consider the questions above from the points of view of both people involved. Then, write down one way the situation could be repaired.

1. Sophia sometimes borrows her older brother Ryan's tablet to watch videos on. One day, she spills a glass of juice on it, and it stops working.

   _____

   _____

2. Madison tells her friend Layla that her mom is moving away to a different city. She asks Layla not to tell anyone. Layla shares Madison's secret with their classmate Zoe.

   _____

   _____

3. Ms. Johnson asks her neighbor Caden to water her garden while she is on vacation. Caden remembers the first day but forgets later in the week. The weather is hot, and several plants die.

   _____

   _____

Think about It

How does apologizing make you a better friend? _____

_____

Answers

p. 11

tina: mother

tamaiti: children

maile: dog

tama: father

p. 12

This image represents making peace, or a treaty.

This image represents a meteor storm. Red ovals represent falling stars, surrounding a black crescent moon.

p. 23

p. 26

p. 28

p. 33

Emmitt is the goalie for their soccer team. Every morning, they get up early to practice with their team. Last week, they blocked a goal at the last second to win the game!

Malia raises chickens in her backyard. Every morning, she lets them out of their coop and makes sure they have enough food and water.

Cai loves cooking. His favorite recipe to make is hot sauce. He even grows his own chili peppers!

p. 35

New York City

LGBTQ and anti-racist causes

Uses social media, gives speeches, and started a charity to provide Christmas presents to transgender youths

p. 47

August 8, 2009

Sonia Sotomayor, President Barack Obama, Chief Justice John G. Roberts Jr.

Sotomayor became the 111th Justice of the Supreme Court.

The Supreme Court Building in Washington, DC

President Barack Obama nominated Sotomayor to the Supreme Court.

Because Sotomayor was the first Hispanic justice to serve on the court and only the third woman to do so

p. 49

Desert

South Sudan

Ethiopia

Ghana

Somalia

Desert

Grassland

p. 54

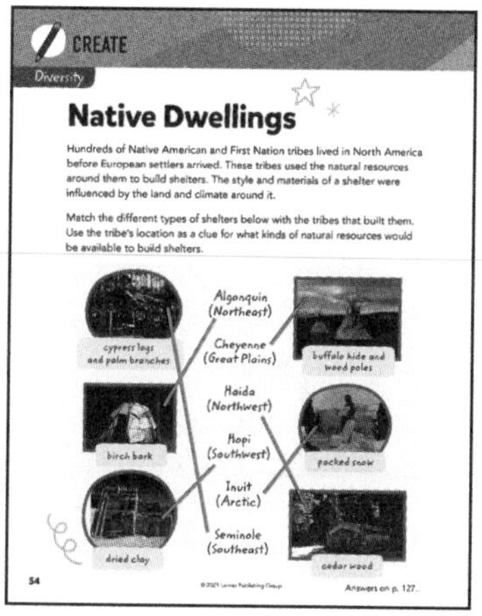

p. 59

January 31, 1919
Jackie Robinson is born.

1939
Robinson began attending college at UCLA.

1945
Robinson joined the Kansas City Monarchs.

1947
Robinson began playing for the Brooklyn Dodgers, making him the first Black player in Major League Baseball in the twentieth century.

1957
Robinson retired from baseball.

1962
Robinson was inducted into the Baseball Hall of Fame.

1963
Robinson and his wife Rachel hosted a jazz concert to raise money for jailed Civil Rights activists.

1964
Robinson co-founded Freedom National Bank.

October 24, 1972
Robinson died.

p. 67

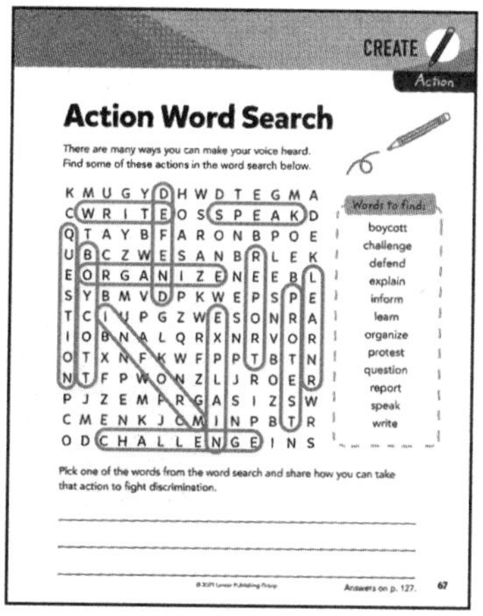

p. 78

1. F

2. O

3. F

4. O

5. F

6. O

p. 91

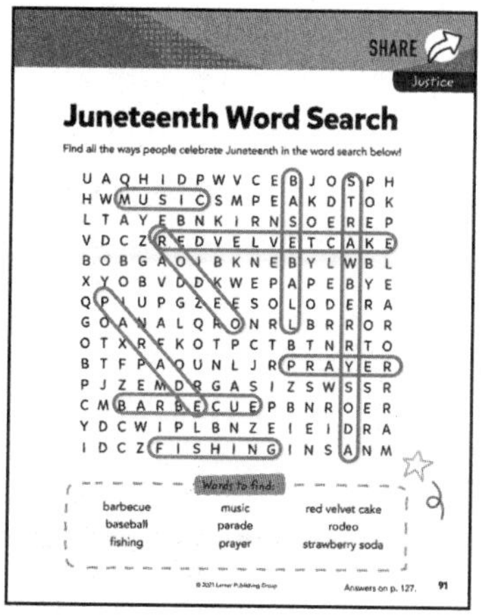

p. 111

A=First Hispanic justice to serve on the US Supreme Court

F=First woman to fly a plane solo across the Atlantic Ocean

C=First Black woman in space

E=First woman to be inducted into the Rock & Roll Hall of Fame

D=First actor who uses a wheelchair to win a Tony Award

B=First Native American to serve in a US president's cabinet

Acknowledgments

The images in this book are used with the permission of: © 4kclips/Shutterstock Images, p. 114; © AFGE/Flickr, p. 110 (Deb Haaland); © AJP/Shutterstock Images, p. 29; © AlasdairJames/iStockphoto, p. 20 (Jasmine Rice); © Anastasia_B/Shutterstock Images, p. 27 (sign icons); © Asier Romero/Shutterstock Images, p. 49 (boy with crossed arms.); © atoss/iStockphoto, p. 20; © AvailableLight/iStockphoto, p. 7; © Barmaleeva/Shutterstock Images, p. 65; © Bastiaan Slabbers/iStockphoto, p. 90; © Bhupi/iStockphoto, p. 124; © Blacqbook/Shutterstock Images, p. 16 (Trinidad Carnival); © BombaySal/Wikimedia Commons, p. 54 (long house); © Brecht Bug/Flickr, p. 80; © Carlos M. Vazquez II/Wikimedia Commons, p. 112; © Cat__Design/iStockphoto, p. 43; © Celso Pupo/Shutterstock Images, p. 18; © CHENG FENG CHIANG/iStockphoto, p. 109; © Chinnapong/Shutterstock Images, p. 116; © david n madden/Shutterstock Images, p. 54 (birch bark wigwam); © Evangelio Gonzalez/Flickr, p. 54 (Seminole Chickee); © faidzzainal/iStockphoto, p. 51; © FatCamera/iStockphoto, p. 76; © Frank E. Kleinschmidt/Wikimedia Commons, p. 54 (igloo); © GlobalStock/iStockphoto, p. 83; © Glynnis Jones/Shutterstock Images, p. 16 (Puerto Rico costume); © Guillermo Kahlo (1871-1941)/Wikimedia Commons, p. 44; © illustrart/iStockphoto, p. 20 (wheat); © Irina Simkina/Shutterstock Images, p. 115; © Jamie Lamor Thompson/Shutterstock Images, p. 118; © Joecho-16/iStockphoto, p. 26 (Grand Canyon); © Joel Levine/Flickr, p. 92; © Joseph Sohm/Shutterstock Images, p. 110 (Aretha Franklin); © kaanates/iStockphoto, pp. 20 (eddoes), 20 (yucca); © kali9/iStockphoto, p. 96; © Kovaleva_Ka/iStockphoto, p. 20 (sweet potato); © Labib Retroman/Shutterstock Images, p. 56 (Nelson Mandela Day illustration); © lev radin/Shutterstock Images, pp. 110 (Ali Stroker), 106; © Mario De Moya F/iStockphoto, p. 17 (Dominican Carnival parade); © mark reinstein/Shutterstock Images, p. 56 (Nelson Mandela); © MF production/Shutterstock Images, p. 123 (social media frame); © Mighty Media, Inc., pp. 23, 85; © Mixmike/iStockphoto, p. 5; © Monkey Business Images/Shutterstock Images, pp. 14, 31, 101; © mtphoto19/iStockphoto, p. 20 (lentils); © narikan/Shutterstock Images, p. 37; © narokzaad/Shutterstock Images, p. 108; © NASA Image and Video Library/Wikimedia Commons, p. 72; © NASA/Wikimedia Commons, p. 110 (Mae Jemison); © National Archives and Records Administration, p. 110 (Amelia Earhart); © National Archives and Records Administration/Flickr, p. 52; © nazar_ab/iStockphoto, p. 11; © nyker/Shutterstock Images, p. 54 (tipi); © Odua Images/Shutterstock Images, p. 50; © PeopleImages/iStockphoto, pp. 70, 121; © Pete Souza/Wikimedia Commons, p. 62; © PeterHermesFurian/iStockphoto, p. 48; © Pictographs of the North Americans Indians/Wikimedia Commons, pp. 12–13; © powerofforever/iStockphoto, p. 26 (Devils Tower); © pushlama/iStockphoto, p. 4; © Pyty/Shutterstock Images, p. 20 (map); © Ridofranz/iStockphoto, p. 97; © Riishede/iStockphoto, p. 26 (geyser); © Sheila Fitzgerald/Shutterstock Images, p. 88; © Shizuko Alexander/iStockphoto, p. 79; © SimonSkafar/iStockphoto, p. 26 (Everglades); © Slanapotam/Shutterstock Images, p. 74; © SolStock/iStockphoto, p. 94; © SoumenNath/iStockphoto, p. 6; © Steve Petteway/Wikimedia Commons, p. 46; © Susan Vineyard/iStockphoto, p. 54 (adobe buildings); © Suzifoo/Shutterstock Images, p. 20 (potatoes); © Van Vechten Collection at Library of Congress/Wikimedia Commons, p. 60; © Wikimedia Commons, pp. 58, 68, 110 (Sonia Sotomayor); © York College ISLGP/Wikimedia Commons, p. 32.

Cover Photos: © FatCamera/iStockphoto (girl with backpack); © monkeybusinessimages/Shutterstock Images (girl doing homework); © Ridofranz /iStockphoto (children doing homework outdoors)

Design Elements: © Devita ayu silvianingtyas/Shutterstock Images (spirals); © Meowlina Meow/Shutterstock Images (hand drawn doodles); © Mighty Media, Inc. (curvy lines); © Nazarkru/Shutterstock Images (abstract background); © OctoPaper/Shutterstock Images (school doodles); © ONYXprj/Shutterstock Images (paper)